DOWNSIZED

How To Survive and Thrive At Your Own Downsizing

Marco Cruz

ISBN: 1461129265
ISBN-13: 9781461129264

To all past, present, and future
downsized employees

Reclaim your life

To my beautiful and beloved wife, Grisel

To my dearest daughter, Gretel

you are always in my heart

The most beautiful sound:

My daughter's uncontrollable laughter

TABLE OF CONTENTS

PUTTING IT ALL TOGETHER

(YOUR STRATEGIC DOWNSIZING SURVIVAL PLAN)

INTRODUCTION

There are only three types of employees at a downsizing company: the ones who have been downsized, the ones being downsized, and the ones about to be downsized. There are no other types, period.

Every year, in fact, for decades now, employees have been downsized, downgraded, rightsized, downscaled, reduced, transformed, cut back, contracted, subcontracted, laid off, and outsourced.

And still it is amazing, just about every day or every week, to hear about employees being shocked about being downsized.

Really? "I didn't see it coming" is a comment often heard. Really? How can this be possible?

It is sad to see employees cry in despair, walk with their heads down, feel defeated, depressed, embarrassed, ashamed, or even kill themselves for being downsized. But why are employees surprised? Why are employees embarrassed and ashamed?

Isn't downsizing a fact of life? It happens almost every day. It definitely happens every year. And for all practical purposes, the prevalent trend indicates downsizings will continue happening in the future.

Downsizing has become a sure thing. It has become certain. Just like death and taxes.

So, can someone please tell all employees at downsizing companies: *if you have not been downsized yet, you will be downsized today or in the near future.*

This book is about taking the fear out of losing your job and what to do about your employment demise before, during, and after you are downsized. Instead, embrace the fact that you will be downsized, understand it, love it, thrive on it, and make it part of your career plan, your employment strategy, and your success in life.

If you work for a company that will try its hardest not to downsize anyone, a company that truly values employees, a company that invests time and money in the development of its employees, a company that provides better salaries and benefits when everybody else around is cutting salaries and benefits, you have arrived at employment heaven.

You should work hard for this company. Arrive at work early and leave late. Don't call in sick. Take work home. Provide the company with your best ideas. Do whatever you can to contribute to help this company succeed. This company is providing you a good job with a decent salary so you can support yourself and your family.

You too should read this book to learn how the rest of us live. You will have a greater appreciation of your job and your employer.

THE BASICS

Make downsizing an essential part of your career plan, part of your success. Again, this is your success, not the company's success. These are two different things, in case you don't remember or you don't know it.

Let's start with the basics. A job is a contract between two parties, the one paying and the one being paid. The one paying (the company) expects something out of the one being paid (the employee).

What does the downsizing company want? Who knows? Who cares anyway if, in the end, you will be downsized? I guess the company expects you to do a job, push a paper from one side to the other. More importantly, the company wants you to conform.

You must conform to the company's directives, mandates, objectives, plans, projects, policies, procedures, wishes, desires, whims, communications, marketing machine, spin, surveys, pilot programs, focus groups, benchmarks, etc. You must conform to all of it, or else, you will be facing the downsizing squad sooner rather than later. Got it?

What do you want? You want at least to be paid for your trouble of showing up every day, for conforming to the law of the company land. And, you want to be left alone...until the day of your downsizing. This is not much to ask, is it?

Never, ever, ever think you are indispensable. You are not. In fact, since the company will downsize you, the company has already made the decision for you. To the company you are dispensable, disposable, and dischargeable. It is not even funny. It's that simple.

HOW TO PLAY THE GAME FROM THE BEGINNING

Don't you love the hiring process? Don't you love the dance? The company wants to pay you the least; you want to be paid the most. This is your moment. This is the time to negotiate for the best salary, extra vacation days, more benefits, cubicle or office size, stationery, and, yes, a lesser workload. This is a one-day opportunity. There are no second chances.

If you can't get anything out of the negotiation, ask the company hiring representative to treat you to lunch. The cheapskate declined? Ask for a cup of coffee, or a bottle of water. You have won something. This is the last time you will see or hear from the representative. Don't bother calling back for instructions or advice; your call will not be answered.

Afterwards, you become part of the institution—institutionalized. It is like many marriages, doomed from the beginning. The best day of the marriage is the wedding day. How can anyone top that?

Want your marriage to last and be good for you and your spouse? Work with your partner to create better and more personally satisfying days after the wedding. Maybe downsizing companies should do just that.

FIRST DAY AT WORK

Your best day at work is the day you are hired. It is all downhill from there. Notice, this has nothing to do with doing any work. Savor your first day at work. Enjoy it. Don't worry about doing any work. You have more important things to do, such as get the lay of the land, begin to draft your next unemployment and reemployment strategy, etc. Remember, your first day at work is the first day on the countdown to your eventual downsizing.

As soon as humanly possible, run to the water cooler. Identify friends and foes. Join the rumor mill to start gathering information on how to survive in this environment.

THE COMPANY

The downsizing company has already decided it is your fault that the company does not achieve its operational and financial goals.

Now, the company is the one who creates and implements the strategic, operational, and financial plans. You just follow the orders. How is it, then, that you get the blame? Well, think about it. Do you think any company in its right mind will admit failure? Do you imagine an executive going to the chief executive officer, the board of directors (the executives' ultimate bosses), or company owners and saying: "I am sorry my strategic plan did not work; we will not make the numbers."

Absolutely not. The company will blame you, current market conditions, the economy, the recession, competition, government regulation, currency fluctuations, pension obligations, or the weather, as the cause for the lack of revenue and the lack of profit. Whatever the company thinks will stick as a justifiable excuse.

Don't forget, the main job of the company decision makers is to make sure they are personally fine, and their personal financial goals and career goals are met.

The executive thought process may be: "I am the smartest and I have worked harder than anyone else in the company." This doesn't sound self-serving, does it? "I am counting on my salary increase and my bonus to meet my very important financial goals. I need to do whatever I have to do to get my money."

The executive has many very important issues to be concerned about: the mansion mortgage payment, the membership to the country club, purchasing a bigger yacht or the newest and biggest car, gifts for the spouse, girlfriend, or boyfriend, the next cruise around the world, etc.

To set the stage for the next round of downsizings, the executives will mention the personnel issues, lack of skills, skill set gaps, entitlement mentality, lack of motivation, inflated salaries, overly generous benefits, excessive pension obligations, whatever works.

Now executives have a different employment contract. Their salaries, bonuses, options, stock grants, vacations, and all other imaginable perks are negotiated before day one. Before they do any work! A two-, three-, five-year-or-more salary, severance, or pension is negotiated ahead of time. If the company or the executive ends the contractual obligation early, the company will pay a handsome severance amount to end the contract, even for gross negligence or failure to meet any and all objectives. This is great deal. How come you can't get the same deal?

Executives have at their disposal a great number of resources to do their jobs. They have many employees report to them. Previous and current plans and strategies are available to them. Hundreds of books have been written about creating and executing strategic and operational plans in many or all industries. Copy and paste, anyone? There are executive conferences available featuring the best experts in the world. An executive is faltering in one area? Executive coaches are available to him or her. An executive does not know how to do a job or doesn't want to be blamed? A consultant can be hired.

Imagine you telling your boss, "I am not sure how to do this part of my job" or "I don't know how to do this job." Most likely you will be fired on the spot.

Try your hardest to become an executive. It is the best deal in town. If not, work on your strategic downsizing survival plan.

THE UNDENIABLE FACTS

In case you don't know or you don't see it, the workplace has changed from lifetime employment to a lifetime of downsizings.

For years, employment experts have been saying company workers should expect to be downsized five to seven times in their lifetime. So, why you don't believe it and accept it? Why not embrace the fact that you will be downsized and make it part of your career and success plans?

THE CASE FOR MEDIOCRITY

Companies breed mediocrity and conformity. Companies want it both ways. On one hand, they want you to work yourself to death for them. On the other hand, they want you to be mediocre and conform to their many rules, policies, and procedures, and their every whim.

Well, which one is it? What do they really want? Where do they put their money? It is very easy to figure out.

Before the beginning of every fiscal year, the company makes two very important decisions: how much money employees will get in the form of raises and bonuses, and what percentage of employees will get better than average, average, and below average increases.

Overall, in the last five to ten years, employees have received an average of 2 percent-3 percent pay increases. Many companies have frozen or forgone increases altogether, and some companies have reduced salaries. The general salary trend all around is downwards. So you may kiss your raise good-bye.

In general, the company will rate 20 percent of employees as above average, 60 percent as average, and 20 percent as below average.

Let's say you make $100,000.00 a year, and the company gives 5 percent or $5,000.00 increases to the top 20 percent, 3 percent or $3,000.00 increases to the average 60 percent, and 1 percent or $1,000.00 increases to the bottom 20 percent of employees.

An employee at the top 20 percent receives an extra $2,000.00 a year, or $166.66 per month, or $38.46 a week, or $7.69 a day.

Don't forget, to be in the top 20 percent, you are required to work extra hard, arrive at work early and leave work late, take work home and work on weekends, miss your kids' games and birthdays, etc.

Aren't you better off skipping the extra $7.69 a day, aiming to be average, arriving at work late and going home early, and spending the weekends with your family? Besides, eventually you will be downsized anyway.

Aren't you better off spending more of your working hours developing and refining your antidownsizing strategy, networking, and targeting or applying for better and higher-paying jobs at other companies?

For an employee, the best and fastest way to make more money is to find another job at another company. There is no need to wait for the twelve-month review.

There are companies reducing, freezing, or eliminating salary increases. And there are companies reducing employee salaries while executives continue to enjoy raises, bonuses, and all the additional perks and benefits. More reason for you to be average and for you to always make your main priority your personal success by focusing on your strategic downsizing survival plan.

WHO IS INCLUDED ON THE DOWNSIZING LIST

Usually, the bottom performers are first on the list of employees to be downsized. More reason for you to be average. It is that simple. This will add months or years to your employed status.

The next on the list are the employees with the worst attendance records. Well, find out in your department the average number of sick days taken by your peers, and limit your sick days to the average for your department, group, or division.

Don't make the easy and obvious attendance mistakes. Do not call in sick on Mondays. Your boss will assume you are an alcoholic, drug addict, or party animal. Don't call in sick on Fridays. Your boss will assume you want to start partying early before the weekend officially begins. Your peers will resent you and probably report you or bad-mouth you for leaving them behind. Don't call with the excuse of having a cold and show up the next day with no signs of sneezing or coughing. Everybody is watching.

The third group on the list used to be the employees with the least seniority. Now, this is rapidly reversing to the opposite. The third group now includes the employees with the most seniority. Find out which criterion your company is using.

When you think about it, it makes sense to downsize the older workers. They make a lot more money, have more vacation time, probably better benefits, and by now are slower, more forgetful, and, worst of all, they are at much higher risk of suffering expensive diseases, heart attacks, strokes, etc. The company has already sucked the best blood out of older workers. It makes sense to get a new batch of younger workers with an ample supply of fresh young blood.

The final group is an all-inclusive group of characters. You are included if your boss or your boss's boss or any of the decision makers don't like you. If you are expected to suck up and you haven't done it, you are included. If you are too tall, too short, too fat, too skinny, too wide, too narrow, too light, or too dark, you are included. Whatever possible reason you can imagine, you may be included in this group. Make sure you stay away from this list if you can, or for as long as you can.

MANAGEMENT

Your boss, like the executives in the company, is concerned with paying the mortgage for the big house, the new car payment, the next family vacation. All the good stuff you don't have. Your boss's main concerns are how to get a bigger raise and bonus, and how to stay away from the downsizing list. Yes, sometimes managers get downsized, too.

The last thing on your boss's mind is you, your raise, or your mortgage payment.

There are three ways to manage your boss: suck up to your boss all the time, to the point of suffocation; suck-up sometimes; or don't suck up at all.

Which way you go depends on your preference, and your boss's personality. Some people like to be sucked up to more than others. Insecure bosses tend to enjoy it a lot more.

Sucking up is an art. It takes a special set of skills and abilities. If you don't know how to do it, learn if necessary.

Why suck up? Because it works. There is something innately human about being praised, even if we don't deserve it. Oh yeah, sometimes it is incredible the opinion that managers have of themselves, and the opinion of everyone around them; if they would only ask.

Sucking up will keep you off of the downsizing list for a while, or maybe for a long while, longer than other better-performing employees for sure.

Sometimes managers call sucking up to them "rapport." They forget rapport is a mutual two-way relationship. Sucking up is only from you to them.

Always get along with your boss. Let your boss know you are a friendly or at least a nonthreatening presence. Do not question, argue, criticize or challenge your boss. Any of these actions will guarantee you a place on the downsizing list.

If you don't get along with your boss, stay out of the way. Your boss is not a morning person? Make yourself invisible in the morning.

Your boss doesn't like you? You are obsessed with trying to find out why? Who cares? Nobody cares. At most companies, it is not written anywhere that your boss is supposed to like you. If you are looking for someone to like you or be nice to you, find it at home with relatives and friends. Besides, it is probably better if your boss doesn't like you. You don't have to fetch coffee or the newspaper, or lower yourself to suck up.

Your boss is not as smart as you are? Or your boss is plain dumb? Leave it alone. Just live with it. Remember, your main goal is to stay off the downsizing list and to work on your strategic plan.

Why? Even if you prove you are smarter, you think the company will admit it made a colossal mistake by promoting your boss? Of course not.

If you have a dumb boss, consider yourself lucky. It will be easier for you to make yourself look good. At least you don't work for the boss from hell.

THE BOSS FROM HELL

Sometimes companies promote someone with zero human relations skills. This is the boss from hell.

Companies could avoid all the stress, aggravation, illnesses, extra cost, lawsuits, Equal Employment Opportunity Commission claims, and loss of productivity if, before promoting or hiring someone, they asked themselves, does this person have any ability to relate to other human beings?

Now there are characters that live a double existence. Or they have intentionally developed a multiple personality disorder. They are the nicest people to their higher-ups. But they are the worst nightmare to anyone at their level or below them.

The company can claim ignorance. But no, the higher-ups should know better, since a few of them already suffer the same disorders.

If you work for a boss from hell, don't say anything, stay out his or her way, transfer to another department, or get another job.

If you report to an abusive boss, deal with it. Immediately let your boss know you are not the victim type. At the first incident, stop your boss in his or her tracks. Abusive bosses are very insecure. If you handle it right, they will leave you alone. They will find another victim. Otherwise, you will suffer terribly for as long as you are there.

An easy way to deal with the abuser is to send the abuser an e-mail. Don't bother going to Human Resources. Your word, the word of your peers, or casual witnesses does not mean much. And words are open to interpretation.

The company's interpretation, which is: you are overreacting, let it go, you are a baby, you are a whiner, and you are wrong.

An e-mail provides a date and time of the abuse, the facts of the abuse, and free electronic backup storage for future reference. Of course, your main storage is the e-mail you will forward to your personal account at home and the printed copies you will keep at home and the office.

A brief e-mail message, keeping with the accepted corporate language guidelines, may be something like this:

Dear beloved boss,

I consider myself so lucky to be working for someone as smart, hardworking, and dedicated as you are. I work very hard every day to live up to your standards.

The reason for my message is to let you know, I don't appreciate you calling me stupid twenty-five times during our meeting in your office today at 3 p.m. I know this must have been an oversight on your part. I need to be sure this is the first and last time something of this nature will happen. This seems to be so out of character coming from you, I am sure this will not happen again.

I truly appreciate your attention to this matter.

Make sure you send the e-mail on Friday afternoon and leave immediately. As soon as the boss from hell reads the e-mail, he or she will come out of the office looking for your blood. You need to make sure you are long gone before this happens. You don't want to be there when the boss from hell punches a couple of walls or throws stuff in the office. Let your boss simmer and cool down over the weekend. He will take out the frustration on a friend or relative. Oh well. Hopefully the company executives will find out who this person really is. Most likely, they already know. If your boss calls, don't answer your telephone.

On Monday, pretend as if nothing happened. The boss from hell will probably pretend that nothing happened, too, or he or she will give you a lame excuse and life will go on. But now, always remember, you just crossed the line. From now on, you will have to walk the straightest possible line. The boss from hell, like a hyena, will be waiting for you to trip or get distracted. Then, the boss from hell will eat you alive while inflicting on you the most possible pain.

If the boss from hell abuses you again, forward him or her the first e-mail with a second warning. This time, copy the HR rep and his or her manager. Your fate is now sealed. You are basically gone at the next downsizing or sooner. Who cares? You were going to be downsized anyway. What is worse? You being abused, humiliated, put down, and insulted every day, or taking the risk to stop the abuse and risking being downsized sooner? It is your choice.

If you call HR, be very careful. Just tell the HR rep to read the e-mail, and tell him or her you want the abuse to stop. Be matter-of-fact. Remember, everything you say will be held against you. Don't be emotional. Most of all, don't cry. There are HR types who hate tears. It is probably the frustrated ones, the ones who did not know what to do with themselves and ended up in HR. Who knows?

HUMAN RESOURCES

If you don't want to be on the downsizing list, don't complain to Human Resources. They don't like it. Like you, your boss, and everybody else, they are busy working, doing other things everybody else is doing, shopping on the Internet, checking the sports pages, gossiping, reading magazines, or, most importantly, worrying about being downsized.

You don't believe me? Ask the IT guy monitoring Internet traffic in the basement.

Don't even call Human Resources to ask Human-Resources-related questions about benefits, vacation, a death in the family, etc.

They are busy. Rub them the wrong way and they will add you to the downsizing list sooner rather than later. Find the answer to your questions somewhere else.

It is amazing how many employees believe Human Resources reps are there to protect the employees against the company. Human Resources reps are paid by the company to implement the rules and regulations according to the company standards, to apply fairness and justice according to the company, and to defend the company at all cost.

Now there are good, hardworking, and dedicated Human Resources representatives. If you have an opportunity, befriend them. They are some of the nicest people you will find there.

But there are many HR reps that don't care or don't want to be bothered. Especially, they don't want to be bothered by you. These HR types are like cops in third world countries. You can never find one when you need one.

But go through a yellow light or throw a candy wrapper on the ground and they will immediately appear out of nowhere to give you a ticket.

SUING THE COMPANY

After being downsized, you think you have a case for age discrimination, or any other type of discrimination? I doubt it. The corporate attorneys will design the downsizing in a way to get around age discrimination or any of the discrimination laws.

Talking about lawyers, you might think you want to sue the company. Really? Think hard before you do it, or don't do it. Don't waste your time.

For starters, the company has a Legal Department full of highly paid lawyers, who, like everyone else, are very concerned about keeping their salaries, paying for the mortgage on the mini-mansion, and supporting their lifestyles. If the company does not have a Legal Department, then the company retains a very expensive law firm to defend the company against employees like you.

The Legal Department also has an annual budget to defend the company against your lawsuit. The company is thinking about and planning for your lawsuit even before you thought about it.

The annual budget could be $1 million, $10 million, $50 million, etc. And if that is not enough money to defend against you, the Legal Department can always tap more millions from the company emergency funds.

Now, how much money do you have to go against the company, $1,000, $5,000, $50,000? Most likely, you don't have enough money.

You will need a lawyer to represent you. You think a lawyer will take your case free of charge? Okay, this is the other issue. Unless you hire a selfless attorney, one of those you see in the movies defending the little guy, a lawyer will want to be handsomely compensated for the trouble of taking your case.

As soon as you meet the lawyer and before you open your mouth, he or she will make a quick calculation as to how much money he or she will get out of you to pay for the mortgage on the mini-mansion, the expensive car, the expensive suits, etc. As soon as you open your mouth, the lawyer will have a better idea of how much money he or she will be making by taking your case.

By the time you are done explaining what the big bad company did to you, the lawyer will know with a great degree of accuracy how much money, if any, your case is worth. See, the lawyer already knows the outcome of a case like yours. You don't.

Then, the lawyer will go about trying to get paid as soon as possible. In most cases, the lawyer will want a retainer, meaning the lawyer will want to get paid before he or she does any work. As soon as you pay that retainer, you can kiss that money good-bye. The money is gone. The lawyer will make sure every penny of that retainer is spent, outcome or no outcome.

Now you have two problems: you have a problem with the company, and you have a problem with your own attorney, who is spending that retainer money faster than you can count.

You have another problem, too. As soon as you sue the company, an army of people will be called to provide information against you: your manager and peers, HR, Security, Compliance, Communications, Benefits, etc. Anyone who was ever in contact with you will be called. Some people will withhold or reluctantly provide information. Some people will be delighted to throw you under the bus. Now all these people have peers, family, and friends. How many of them do you think will keep this to themselves?

If you want to get something to feel vindicated, have your lawyer file a complaint or contact the company. The company will soon make a low-ball offer. Try to get your attorney to get the company to offer its "make-you-go-away" settlement amount. This is the amount companies offer to make you go away, regardless of the merits of your complaint. The amount could be $1,000, $10,000, etc. Take the offer and move on with your life.

By the way, never call your attorney to vent or to chat. The attorney will be charging you the hourly rate to pretend to be listening to you.

You still want to go ahead and sue the company, because you are angry, insulted, or the company violated your rights or principles? Do yourself a favor: go to the courthouse library and read up on cases like yours. Find out how long the cases take from beginning to end, what the settlements are like, what the judges records are.

Try contacting others like you who sued the company and went to court. What was the emotional toll? In the end, was it worth it?

Lastly, by suing the company you are at risk of becoming unemployable in your industry or anywhere. Everything is confidential? Yeah, but somehow, many times, other people "confidentially" find out you were involved in a lawsuit against your company.

If your manager, the company, or both grossly discriminated against you or violated your rights, you may just have found your ticket to your early retirement.

See, if you had a downsizing strategy from day one, you would not be angry. You would have been working for yourself all along. You would not be upset. You would be going home happy that you knew all along this would be the outcome and that you spent all your time working on polishing and perfecting your downsizing strategy.

IT IS A JUNGLE OUT THERE

Have you ever watched on TV a herd of zebras happily grazing on the great plains of Africa? I ask if you have watched it on TV because most of us can't afford to vacation in Africa. We don't get paid enough. When is the last time you heard one of your co-workers say, "I just came back from a safari in Africa." If you have heard it, most likely you are making a lot of money. Good for you.

Anyway, it is a beautiful day in Africa. The sun is out. The sky is blue. It is not hot or humid. The grass is fresh and delicious. The zebras are happily feasting, wagging their tails. There are birds and gazelles around them. Everybody is happily living together. It looks like a scene from paradise or the garden of Adam and Eve.

All of a sudden, a pack of lions jumps out of nowhere. In less than a second, the herd runs away at a great speed. There is a lot of confusion, a cloud of dust covers part of the herd, then, one or two zebras fall to the ground. A lion has grabbed a zebra by the throat, while another has jumped on her back. Sensing an untimely death, the zebra kicks and lets out the most eerie and scary death screams, hopelessly. Her eyes are wildly open. The lion holding her throat lets the zebra watch as another lion tears chunks of her flesh apart, as if to ensure the zebra suffers greatly before her death. Finally, the lion cuts her throat, and the zebra dies. This has lasted just a few seconds. In a few minutes the zebra is gone. The lions feast on the best meats. Then the hyenas and vultures finish the remains.

This is what a downsizing feels like to unsuspecting employees.

Now herd dynamics prior to and during the attack are very similar to employee behaviors. If you look closely, most zebras, like many employees, seem to be unaware of the impending attack. A few of them even get closer to the lions, without realizing danger is just a few feet away.

There are zebras always staying in front of the herd. These are like employees that sense or fear an attack, but don't know what to do. Other zebras stay at the back of the herd. These are like employees who have resigned themselves to their demise. We all have seen the employees who come to work and bury their heads in their work or their monitors like ostriches burying their head in the sand, hoping the corporate predators will not find them.

Other zebras are grazing in the middle of herd. When they fall behind, they take a few steps forward and place themselves back in the middle of the herd. Every few minutes, these zebras lift their heads, take a look around, and go back to grazing. These are like the employees who have a strategic downsizing survival plan. They know the downsizing is eventually coming. But they know what to do, before, during, and after the downsizing.

During the attack, there are zebras that run as fast as possible, outrunning everybody else. They look scared and confused. These zebras risk injuring themselves, spraining or breaking a leg. They will be easy pickings for the lions on the next attack.

These zebras are like the employees that run around during or after a downsizing talking to management, HR, or whoever will listen to them, saying how scared they are and how much they need their job, pleading with management to give them more work, or backstabbing their peers to ensure they don't get downsized. They are only making it easier for the corporate predators.

Other zebras stay towards the middle of the pack, watching all around for any surprises. They are not galloping too fast or too slow. As soon as the lions have their prey, these zebras immediately go back to grazing. They are like employees with a strategic plan. They are not scared or surprised. This is just the way it is at the downsizing company.

As the corporate predators like to say, "This is not personal, just business." The funny part is, when it happens to them, they scream and wail like pigs. They complain and sue and demand much more on the way out; but wasn't it "just business"? Go figure.

There are zebras behind the middle of the pack not running at full speed, but intentionally blocking the zebras behind them. These zebras know they don't have to outrun the lions. They only have to outrun the zebras behind them. By blocking the other zebras, they ensure they don't get kill themselves. It is a jungle out there, after all.

These zebras are like the employees who spend their time backstabbing other employees, serving their heads to management and HR. These employees befriend management or find the perfect moment to bad-mouth you and everybody else. They may be subtle and tell management something like this: "My co-worker (meaning you) is so nice, so hardworking, a pleasure to be around, but…" And here it comes, the stab to the heart, to make sure you are the next on the list and not them. Or, they may be more direct and say, "My co-worker and I were in a meeting, and I am very concerned about my co-worker's comments, and, to be honest with you, I am concerned with her skills and abilities to do the job, because…" And here we go again; you are next on the list.

When the lions are hungry or need a lot of meat, they send a couple of lions in front of the herd and a couple of lions towards the middle. Then, the rest of the pack launches an attack from the back of the herd. Zebras from all sides of the herd fall victims to this attack.

Just like the lions, sometimes the corporate predators conduct an all-out attack. This time all types of employees fall prey to this attack, including the ones with a survival strategy, good, bad, and indifferent. Everyone gets a downsizing day.

D-DAY
(DOWNSIZING DAY)

So today is the day. If you have a downsizing strategy and you have been paying attention, you already know it. This is the time of the year, this is the preferred quarter, the last quarter was the worst ever, etc. If you don't know the exact date, you can sense it. You can smell it. You feel the corporate predators approaching from behind, setting up the ambush, ready for the kill.

There is an eerie calm in the hallways. Unsuspecting employees are going about their business. Suspecting employees are on guard, pretending the best way they can that everything is fine.

Conspiracy theory employees, well-informed employees, and the ones that need to know everything, have been briefing you with the latest rumors, executive meetings and movements, Human Resources meetings and movements, number of executives in the building, more or new security guards on the premises, etc.

Based on your research, you know what to expect at your downsizing meeting: severance amount, benefits, outplacement, etc. You are ready. You have interviewed previously downsized employees and have a very good idea about what goes on at the meeting. You have a pen, your questions written down on a pad or index card, and you carry them with you at all times. You are calm, cool, and collected. You are ready to go.

As soon as you get called to the meeting, grab a cup of coffee, juice, or glass of water. Better yet, always have a bottle of water ready with you. A sip of water can help you calm down during the meeting, or it can help you pause to think before you ask or answer a question.

Make sure you are professional and polite and immediately develop rapport with who-ever is in the room. Your boss may be there, read you a script, hand you over to the HR rep, and leave, or there may be someone you have never seen before. It doesn't matter. Let them know you understand and are fine with their decision.

Let them conduct their meeting. You will have time for questions later. Make sure you listen and understand what they are saying. They probably will give you a written downsizing notice or agreement confirming the details of your downsizing. Take your pad or index card out and check that all your questions and concerns are answered.

Now is your turn to negotiate. You have already decided on your negotiation strategy. It may be matter-of-fact; it may be in the form of an appeal, etc. Those of you that can cry on demand, this may be the best time to do it to get what you want. Just don't overdo it. It may backfire on you.

You already know what you want or what you need. You may need additional months of medical insurance due to illness, additional outplacement, vacation time or severance, a laptop to search for jobs, use of your voice mail, etc. Even if you don't get anything else, it is worth asking.

Make sure you end the meeting on the best possible terms. Your next job may come from your former boss, the HR rep, or someone you know within the company.

As soon as you are done with the meeting, execute the job search part of your strategy. Your resume and cover letter are ready. You have been networking inside and outside the company for months. You have been in touch with a solid number of peers and colleagues. You have been attending industry conferences and job fairs.

Immediately, personally reach out to each of your top ten or twenty contacts. Let them know you have been downsized and you are in the market looking for a new job. Ask them to send your way any or as many leads as they may have.

Send a message requesting job leads from all your friends and acquaintances on LinkedIn, Facebook, Twitter, or any other social network site.

Okay, if you want to take one hour, one day, or one week to feel sorry for yourself, go ahead. After all, we are all human. Maybe you want to crawl in bed and lay there in a fetal position for a couple of days and cry. Maybe you want to get really drunk one night. Maybe you want to eat a chocolate cake for twelve people by yourself. Go ahead, take it out of your system, but then hit the road. It is time to get a new job.

Don't hide. Don't be ashamed or embarrassed. Don't be like those people who store their car in the garage and hide in their homes during the day, or the people that dress up every morning and spend the day at a relative's home so the neighbors don't find out they are out of work.

This is not personal. This is business, your business. This is about you and your family surviving and fighting like hell to have a decent life. This is no time to hide. This is a fight for survival. Tell all your neighbors, the dry-cleaning person, the gas attendant, everyone you come in contact with; tell them you are in the market looking for a job. You never know who will give you your next lead.

PUTTING IT ALL TOGETHER
(YOUR STRATEGIC DOWNSIZING SURVIVAL PLAN)

Throughout the book, you have been reading about your strategic downsizing survival plan. But what is the plan? If you don't have a plan, read on and create your own plan. Any plan is better than no plan.

By the way, this plan applies at any stage of the downsizing wheel. Whether you are employed or already downsized, start your plan immediately. It will make your life easier, and it will free you from the downsizing chain, because the downsizing company's plan is to get rid of you anyway.

Your ultimate goal is for you to leave the downsizing company and find yourself a job in a company interested in an honest and fair employment relationship with you.

YOUR OWN ASSESSMENT

Well, if you are employed, start by asking yourself, how is the company doing? Is it doing good or bad? How is the demand for the products and competition? How long ago were the last two or three downsizings? What is the chance there will be a downsizing soon? What is the chance you will get down-sized this time? How do you stack up against your peers in terms of attendance, age, per-formance, all other areas, or the sucking-up factor?

Read the company operation plans, executive announcements, stock price and performance, etc. The company will not openly announce the downsizing. But read between the lines. Ask your peers and co-workers. Ask your supervisor or manager, what are the chances of a downsizing soon? They will not tell you, even if they know it. But pay attention to their body language and tone of voice. The answer is there. Listen, listen, listen, and pay attention; there are so many clues all around you. Some are out in the open, other clues are more subtle.

Have there been any significant changes in your manager's behavior towards you? Does your manager have a problem looking you in the eye, or is your manager avoiding you? Has your manager lost interest on your projects? Or, is your manager not pressing you as much as he or she used to do? Have some or most of your responsibilities been taken away? Have you been recently transferred to another department or group? Are you not invited to meetings? Are there others in the know who are looking at you differently, maybe more sympathetically or with pity?

Are your enemies of all a sudden happy to see you and talking to you? Oh, yes, they want to be close to you, like the lion clenching the zebra's throat; they want to be very close to you when you die. They want to relish your demise to feel better about themselves and their miserable and despicable lives. Has anyone come to you out of nowhere and asked, How are you? Are you okay? Listen and pay attention. No need to be paranoid, but pay attention.

Once you have made your own assessment, calculate how many more days or months you have at the company. Ask yourself: is there anything you can do to avoid the next downsizing? Are there any minor adjustments you can do? Probably not, but it is worthwhile exploring for about five minutes. Don't forget, most of your energy and time should be spent on the other parts of your plan.

From now and on, conduct this assessment every month, or every other month. Include other factors and make adjustments as conditions change. This is your best forecasting tool.

YOUR RESUME

Your resume, cover letter, introduction letter, CV, employment record, qualifications, etc., should always be ready. Obviously, your resume should be the best that lands on a recruiter's desk.

There are now hundreds of books and thousands of Internet sites full of tips and recommendations on how to write resumes and cover letters. If you don't know or can't write it yourself, have a friend do it for you. Or, have a professional write your resume for you.

You must be a professional interviewer. Once or twice a year, you should interview for a job that interests you, or you should interview for a job you already know you don't want just to practice your interview skills. You know which companies are the best to practice your interview skills? The downsizing companies. You don't want to work for them anyway.

NETWORKING

The second part of the plan is networking. Most likely your next job will come from your network of peers and colleagues. Have you been networking inside and outside the company? How many friends or colleagues do you have in your field, industry, or area of expertise? Do you have any mentors or quasi-mentors? How many recruiters are part of your network? Don't you think you should have one or two of those? Their job is to get people like you another job. Have you joined any industry groups? Do you attend professional conferences, not only for the food, entertainment, or to get out the office, but to meet new friends and contacts who potentially will find you a new job?

You should have at least one hundred contacts. Out of the hundred, you may get ten leads. Out of the ten leads, you may get your next job at a good company. It is that simple. If you get a job at a downsizing company, well, you know what to do now.

You should be regularly in touch with your top ten to twenty contacts. This includes correspondence, telephone calls, and going out together. Yes, this is a lot of work. But it beats being home without a job, feeling sorry for yourself.

More reason to be average or below average at the downsizing company, this should give you one or two hours a day for networking. More importantly, not too many people want to be your networking partner when you are unemployed. You just don't have much to offer.

Remember, one out of ten or twenty people will answer your telephone calls when you are unemployed. Yes, get used to the idea.

You should be in touch monthly or quarterly with your other networking peers, exchanging ideas, leads, jokes, etc. And if any one of your networking peers is unemployed or looking for a job, you should spend a good amount of time and effort helping him or her. Remember, tomorrow could be your turn. The best way to receive is to give first.

YOUR FINANCIAL SITUATION

How long can you survive without a job, a month? Two months? A year? You should know exactly how long. This is extremely important. It may take you from a month to more than a year to find another job.

Do you have any savings? Will you get any severance or unemployment, and for how long? Will this be enough to cover your basic needs?

Are you living paycheck to paycheck? I don't care if you are making $20,000 or $200,000 a year. You are at great risk to go through a lot of emotional and physical pain. Are you living beyond your means? Add to the pain the fact that you are lying to yourself and your family. It is that simple: you are living a lie.

Start changing your financial situation today, wherever you are in the downsizing spiral. You should have saved at least a year's worth of living expenses. You don't think so? Ask anyone who has been unemployed, or anyone who has been five days in the hospital, how much money you should have for emergencies.

Money runs out quickly when you are unemployed. It is basic cash flow. It is money coming in (your salary) against money going out (your expenses). If you don't have a job, zero money is coming in, and a lot of money is going out.

If you don't have any savings, take drastic measures immediately. Put your house up for sale today. If you rent, move to a smaller house or apartment.

Organize a tag sale and sell half the stuff you own. You will get a much better price when you do it on your own time. When you are desperate and running out of money, you will sell everything for half the price or a lot less.

You may lose the house, or your car may be repossessed. Debt collectors will be knocking at your door. As someone said, *"If you think no one cares about you, try missing a couple of payments."* The debt collector will be your best and only friend.

You have five or more TVs in the house. Really? You signed up for five thousand channels. Really? How many channels can you watch at the same time or in one night? You have two cars, one for the weekends, and a motor cycle. Really? Think how much you will enjoy that stuff when you don't have a job or money for gas and you can't make the mortgage payment. Sell everything you don't need today.

Now, if you have a year's worth of expenses saved, no debt, and you want to have stuff, go for it. Buy the stuff cash. It is a whole different ball game, as long as you keep adding to your emergency savings.

FAMILY AND FRIENDS

Finally, work hard at having good and strong relationships with family and friends. They are the only ones who will pick you up when you are down. They will help you go through the hard times.

They will listen to you. They will cry with you. They will support you and help you. They will call their friends and try to get you a job. If nothing else, they will visit you or invite you over. They will be there for you.

CONCLUSION

There you have it. That is a basic, strategic, downsizing survival plan. Create your own plan. Do what works for you. Add or take away items as necessary. But, most importantly, have a plan. Remember the zebra. If you don't have a plan, the downsizing company has a plan for you.

Good luck.

To share your stories, or for any questions or comments, write me at downsizedtoday@ gmail.com.